This book
was presented

to <u>MELINA SANCHEZ CORONA.</u>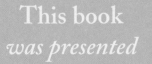

by <u>NORMA LYDIA ACEVES VILLASEÑOR.</u>

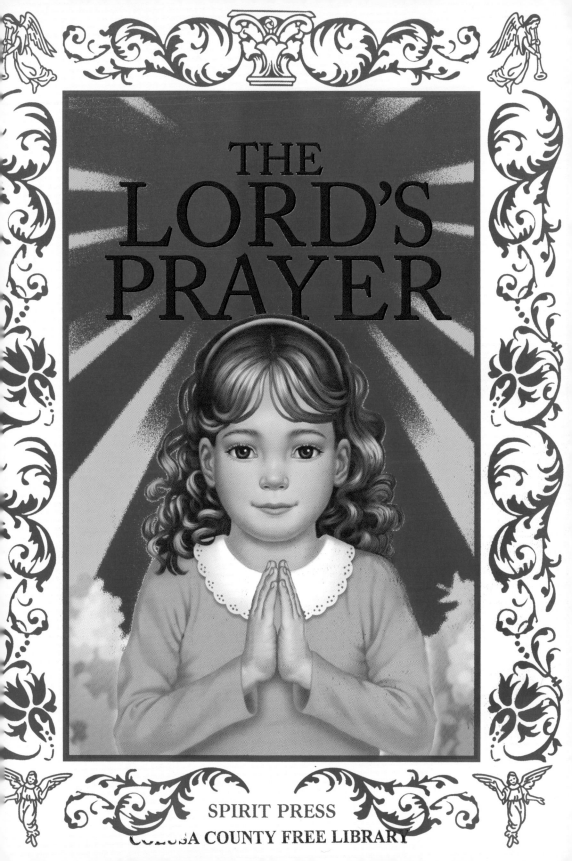

THE LORD'S PRAYER

SPIRIT PRESS

Our Father, who art in heaven, Hallowed be thy name.

Thy
kingdom
come.

Thy will
be done,
on earth,
as it is
in heaven.

Give us
this day
our daily
bread.

And forgive
us our
trespasses,
as we forgive
those who
trespass
against us.

And lead us not into temptation, but deliver us from evil:

For thine is
the kingdom,
and the power,
and the glory,
for ever.
AMEN

FROM MATTHEW 6

And it came to pass, that, after Jesus had prayed,
one of his disciples said to him,
"Lord, teach us to pray."

And Jesus instructed them to pray
with a humble heart of love for God and others.

He taught them to pray in private,
and not make a show of their reverence for God.

He taught that God is not impressed with clever words;
that God hears the simple prayer of a sincere heart.

"For your Heavenly Father knoweth
what things ye have need of, before ye ask him."

THE LORD'S PRAYER

After this manner therefore pray ye:

Our Father who art in heaven,

Hallowed be thy name.

Thy kingdom come. Thy will be done

on earth, as it is in heaven.

Give us this day our daily bread.

And forgive us our trespasses,

as we forgive those who trespass against us.

And lead us not into temptation,

but deliver us from evil:

For thine is the kingdom, and the power,

and the glory, for ever.

Amen.

THE LORD'S PRAYER

Copyright © 2004 by Spirit Press, an imprint of Dalmatian Press, LLC

All rights reserved

SPIRIT PRESS and DALMATIAN PRESS are trademarks
of Dalmatian Press, LLC, Franklin, Tennessee 37067.
ISBN: 1-40371-000-7
13585-0804

Printed in the U.S.A.

05 06 07 08 LBM 10 9 8 7 6 5 4 3